The Rosary

Author: Anonymous

Produced by Michael Gray, Archdiocese of
Portland in Oregon

NIHIL OBSTAT
ARTHURIUS L. McMAHON, O.P., S.T.M
Prior Provincialis

IMPRIMATUR
✠EDUARDUS J. HANNA
Archepiscopus S. Francisci

S. Francisci, die 27 Sept. 1915

NATAL PUBLISHING LLC
ARS LONGA, VITA BREVIS

THE ROSARY

THE name Rosary signifies a crown of roses; and well does this devotion deserve, by just right, a name so beautiful. The rose is the most beautiful of flowers and ravishes our senses with its beauty and perfume; and there is no delight that can equal the heavenly enchantment of the spiritual sweetness which is exhaled from this beautiful prayer.

The Rosary is a spiritual garland of mystic roses with which we deck the brow of Mary—a diadem which reflects the joy and brilliance, the purity and fecundity of the glorious *Queen of Heaven.*

The flowers which we weave are not of this earth, but are indigenous to Paradise, and were transplanted by an angel's hand from their native soil to bloom and flourish among the weeds and thistles of this miserable and sinful world.

There is no form of prayer more efficacious, or more excellent and acceptable before Heaven than Mary's own devotion, the Rosary. There is nothing that the great Holy Father, Pope Leo XIII, urged more upon the Church than the devout practice of reciting the beads in her honor.

The devotion of the Holy Rosary was revealed to St. Dominic by the Blessed Virgin Mary, who commanded him to preach it throughout the world; and hence the Rosary has ever been the spiritual heritage and distinct property of the Dominican Order.

The Rosary is adapted to the learned and the ignorant, and to every capacity. The form and matter are intelligible to the most illiterate, and yet so sublime as to be matter of contemplation worthy of the highest intellect. Moreover, the Rosary is not only a most sublime and perfect devotion, but there is no devotion in the Church which is enriched with more precious and valuable helps to salvation; and there is nothing, outside the Holy Sacrifice, that can profit the living and the dead equal to the pious recitation of the Rosary.

The Form and Matter of the Rosary

The Rosary consists in the recitation, in honor of the Most Holy Virgin Mary, Mother of God, of the Angelic Salutation one hundred and fifty times, distributed into fifteen decades; each decade being preceded by the Lord's Prayer and accompanied by meditation on one of the principal mysteries of our Divine Saviour and terminated by the doxology or "Glory be to the Father," etc. The vocal prayer is the matter, the *body* of this exercise; the meditation on the fifteen mysteries is the form, and, as it were, the *soul* of this prayer. The Rosary is divided into three parts; each part contains five mysteries and is called a chaplet. The first part consists of the five joyful mysteries; the second, of the five sorrowful; and the third, of the five glorious mysteries.

Manner of Reciting the Rosary

The method of reciting the Rosary practiced by the Dominicans is as follows:

In the name of the Father, etc.
V. Hail Mary, full of grace, the Lord is with thee.
R. Blessed art thou among women, and blessed is the fruit of thy womb, Jesus.
V. Thou, O Lord, wilt open my lips.
R. And my tongue shall announce Thy praise.
V. Incline unto my aid, O God.
R. O Lord, make haste to help me.
Glory be to the Father, etc., Alleluia. (From Septuagesima to Easter, instead of Alleluia, say Praise be to Thee, O Lord, King of eternal glory.)

Then announce either "the first part of the holy Rosary, the five joyful mysteries," or "the second part of the holy Rosary, the five sorrowful mysteries," or "the third part of the holy Rosary, the five glorious mysteries." Then the first mystery, "The Annunciation," etc., and Our Father once, Hail Mary ten times, Glory be to the Father once; in the meantime, meditating on the mystery. After reciting each decade is said the Fatima

Prayer:

O my Jesus, forgive us our sins, save us from the fires of hell, and lead all souls to Heaven, especially those in most need of Thy mercy.

After reciting five decades, the Hail, Holy Queen is said, followed by

V. Queen of the most holy Rosary, pray for us.

R. That we may be made worthy of the promises of Christ.

Let Us Pray

O God, whose only begotten Son, by His life, death and resurrection, has purchased for us the rewards of eternal life, grant, we beseech Thee, that, meditating upon these mysteries of the most holy Rosary of the Blessed Virgin Mary, we may imitate what they contain and obtain what they promise. Through the same Christ our Lord. Amen.

The Five Joyful Mysteries

(Assigned for Mondays and Thursdays throughout the year, the Sundays in Advent and after Epiphany till Lent.)

Like scenes of some wondrous drama these Mysteries set before us the joys of the life of our Saviour. One by one the scenes are unfolded—each telling its story, conveying its Gospel lesson to the human soul. Before our mental view pass the personages mentioned in God's Book. Here are Mary the humble, Joseph the obedient, Elizabeth the prayerful, Simeon the just, the angels on earth and in heaven—all bending in lowly reverence before Jesus, the grand central figure of the Rosary devotion. Our minds filled with Faith and Hope and Love, we begin the decades:

First Joyful Mystery:

"The Annunciation"

"And the angel being come in, said unto her: Hail, full of grace, the Lord is with thee; blessed art thou among women. Who having heard, was troubled at his saying, . . . And the angel said to her: Fear not, Mary, for thou hast found grace with God. Behold thou shalt conceive in thy womb, and shalt bring forth a son; and thou shalt call His name Jesus." (St. Luke, I, 28-31)

Mary's Humility

As Jesus, the Savior of Mankind, humbled himself, becoming obedient even unto the death of the Cross, how fitting that Mary, his Mother, should in the moment of her greatest exaltation teach us the lesson of Humility.

Pride wrought the ruin of legions of angels; through pride our first parents sinned in the Garden of Happiness. By humility our salvation was achieved—the humility of the Word of God. In our pride we have disobeyed God's holy law. Through humble penance are we to regain God's favor.

O Mary, humble hand-maid of the Lord, pray that we know our own unworthiness!

Second Joyful Mystery:

"The Visitation"

"And Mary rising up in those days, went into the hill country with haste into a city of Judea. And she entered into the house of Zachary and saluted Elizabeth. And it came to pass, that when Elizabeth heard the salutation of Mary, the infant leaped in her womb."—(St. Luke, I, 39-41.)

Brotherly Love

Charity prompts Mary to visit her cousin Elizabeth in the hour of her need. Ah, how the loving heart of our dear Mother anticipates the words of her Divine Son: "By this shall all men know that you are My disciples, that you have love one for another."

"I was sick and in prison and you did visit Me," says our Saviour. And He calls those specially blessed of His Father who shall feed the hungry, clothe the naked, and bring comfort to those that mourn. Wheresoever we move on earth let us, by kindly word and sympathetic action, bring a warm breath of heavenly charity.

O Mary, sweet Mother of charity, teach us to be kind; and for the sake of Christ to lighten the burden of Christ's least brethren!

Third Joyful Mystery:

"The Nativity"
"And she brought forth her first-born Son, and wrapped Him in swaddling clothes, and laid Him in a manger; because there was no room for them in the inn."—(St. Luke, II, 7.)

Poverty
"Wrapped in swaddling clothes and laid in a manger" is Jesus on the night of His birth. The world had forgotten the richness of being poor. It was needful that Jesus should enter into the world in poverty to teach the lesson of detachment from earthly things. In the Crib of Bethlehem, as from the Mount, Christ teaches the self-same lesson: "Blessed are the poor in spirit, for theirs is the Kingdom of Heaven."

If we possess worldly goods, let us act as God's faithful stewards, giving liberally to the poor of Christ; if poverty be our lot, let us not murmur against God's Holy will, but rather thank God we are saved from the many temptations of riches.

Mary, lover of poverty, teach us to seek first the Kingdom of God.

Fourth Joyful Mystery:

"The Presentation"

"And after the days of her purification, according to the law of Moses, were accomplished, they carried Him to Jerusalem, to present Him to the Lord. As it is written in the law of the Lord: Every male opening the womb shall be called holy to the Lord."—(St. Luke, II, 22, 23.)

Purity

In obedience to the Mosaic law, to which He was not subject, Christ allowed Himself to be presented body and soul in the Temple to teach us that by purity of body and soul we are to consecrate ourselves to the service of God.

"Blessed are the clean of heart, for they shall see God." As we are pure of heart, so will our vision of the things of God be clear. By prayer and the Sacraments shall we maintain purity of life. Prayer will keep our minds in touch with God. Strict examination of conscience will make known to us our faults. The Sacrament of Penance will cleanse our souls. If through the Sacrament of the Eucharist we abide in Christ, Christ will abide in us and keep us pure.

O Mary, Virgin Mother, protect us in body and soul!

Fifth Joyful Mystery:

"The Finding in the Temple"

"And it came to pass, that, after three days, they found Him in the temple, sitting in the midst of the doctors, hearing them and asking them questions. . . . And His mother said to Him: Son, why hast thou done so to us? behold Thy father and I have sought Thee sorrowing. And He said to them: How is it that you sought me? Did you not know that I must be about my Father's business?"—(St. Luke, II, 46, 48, 49.)

Zeal for Souls

Zeal to be about the things that are His Father's prompts Jesus to remain in the pulpit in the midst of the doctors of the law, hearing them and asking them questions. "They that instruct many to justice shall shine as stars for all eternity." (Daniel XII, 3.) How glorious the reward of those who sacrifice themselves for the salvation of souls!

Whatsoever be our station in life, we can work for God by word and example. If our words are holy and of good repute, and our actions are prompted by charity, justice and purity, we are spreading the Gospel of Christ—carrying His message to them that sit in darkness and in the shadow of death.

O Mary, zealous lover of souls, teach us to work for God!

The Five Sorrowful Mysteries

(For Tuesdays and Fridays throughout the year, and the Sundays in Lent)

The curtain has fallen on the Joyful Mysteries to rise slowly again, disclosing the principal scene in the Tragedy of Christ. There is this difference between every other tragedy played out on the wide stage of the earth and the Tragedy of Christ, that each one of us acted a sad part in making our Divine Saviour suffer. When sorrow for our sins brings tears of humble repentance to our eyes, let us still look up to the Cross—the Symbol of Hope. "And I, if I be lifted up from the earth, will draw all things to myself." (St. John, XII, 32.) Saints have meditated on the sufferings of Christ and have found therein the motive for further battling against temptation; sinners have contemplated the Sorrowing Christ and have experienced the undying truth of His words: "Come to Me all you that labor and are burdened, and I will refresh you." (St. Matt. II, 28.)

First Sorrowful Mystery:

"The Agony in the Garden"

"Then Jesus came with them into a country place which is called Gethsemane; and He said to His disciples: Sit you here, till I go yonder and pray . . . And going a little further, He fell upon His face, praying, and saying: My Father, if it be possible, let this chalice pass from me. Nevertheless, not as I will, but as Thou wilt."—(St. Matt., XXVI, 36-39.)

Confidence in Prayer

In agony Christ prayed: "Father, all things are possible to thee; remove this chalice from me; but not what I will, but what thou wilt." (St. Luke, XIV, 36.) Three times He sent up the self-same cry to His Eternal Father, with earnestness and in resignation to the Will of His Father.

Our Saviour, who had a right to be heard because of His reverence, was constant and humble in prayer, whilst we who have so frequently rebelled against God's will pray with distraction and coldness.

O Mary, for whom thy Son didst work a miracle in answer to prayer, pray for us and teach us how to pray earnestly and humbly!

Second Sorrow Mystery:

"The Scourging at the Pillar"

"But the chief priests and ancients persuaded the people, that they should ask Barabbas, and make Jesus away. And the governor answering, said to them: Whether will you of the two to be released unto you? But they said, Barabbas. . . . Then he released to them Barabbas, and having scourged Jesus, delivered Him unto them to be crucified."—(St. Matt., XXVII, 20, 21, 26.)

Hatred of Pleasure

To a world gone mad in the pursuit of pleasure, Christ from the pillar seems to say: "Learn of Me." Standing quivering under the cruel lashes, what a lesson of mortification Christ teaches! Is not every gaping wound in His Sacred Body a rebuke to us who seek to indulge ourselves at all costs—even the cost of our eternal salvation. As we watch the scourging of our Saviour let us bemoan our sins, especially our sins of sensuality.

O Mary, Mother of Sorrows, preach to us anew the sermon of St. Paul, who chastised his body and brought it under subjection. "Know you not that your members are the temple of the Holy Ghost who is in you, whom you have from God; and you are not your own? For you are bought with a great price. Glorify and bear God in your body." (I Cor. VI, 19.)

Third Sorrowful Mystery:

"The Crowning With Thorns"

"Then the soldiers of the governor taking Jesus into the hall, gathered together unto Him the whole band; and stripping Him, they put a scarlet cloak about Him. And platting a crown of thorns, they put it upon His head, and a reed in His right hand. And bowing the knee before Him, they mocked Him, saying: Hail, king of the Jews."—(St. Matt., XXVII, 27-29.)

Humble Faith

"Amen I say to you, unless you be converted, and become as little children, you shall not enter into the Kingdom of Heaven." (St. Matt. XVIII, 2, 3.) How many times through life has Christ taught the lesson of unquestioning faith! He endures the cruel Crowning of Thorns that we may learn to be humble of intellect. Our earth-bound minds can not measure the things of God, nor solve His mysteries.

With simple faith let us accept the truths God has been pleased to reveal of Himself, praying: "I do believe, Lord: Help my unbelief." (St. Mark IX, 23.)

O Mary, pray that our faith may be enlivened!

Fourth Sorrowful Mystery:

"The Carrying of the Cross"

"And they took Jesus, and led Him forth. And bearing His own cross, He went forth to that place which is called Calvary, but in Hebrew Golgotha."—(St. Sohn XIX, 16, 17.)

"And as they led Him away, they laid hold of one Simon of Cyrene, coming from the country; and they laid the cross on him to carry after Jesus."—(St. Luke, XXIII, 26.)

Patience under Trials

"If any man will follow me, let him deny himself, and take up his Cross and follow me. For whosoever will save his life shall lose it; and whosoever shall lose his life for my sake and the gospel, shall save it." (St. Mark VIII, 34.) True discipleship of Christ is shown by the patience with which we endure our trials. Mark the life of Christ! In sorrow He entered into this world; in sorrow He lived; enduring an agony of sorrow He died.

We wish to follow in His footsteps. Let us accept our trials in humility. We have deserved them for our sins.

O Mary, Mother of Sorrows, teach us to bear the Cross with patience!

Fifth Sorrowful Mystery:

"The Crucifixion"

"And they came to the place that is called Golgotha, which is the place of Calvary. . . . And after they had crucified Him they divided His garments, casting lots; that it might be fulfilled which was spoken by the prophet, saying: They divided My garments among them; and upon My vesture they cast lots. And they put over His head His cause written: This is Jesus the King of the Jews."—(St. Matt., XXVII, 33, 35, 37.)

Love of the Cross

"I have a baptism wherewith I am to be baptized; and how am I straitened until it be accomplished." (St. Luke XII, 50.)

How strange that the Saviour should sigh for the culmination of His agony—seek in death His triumph! Our human nature shrinks from pain. Yet if our lives are to be Christ-like, we must rather seek to suffer as Christ has taught us by His life of sorrow.

Trials must surely enter into our lives. 'Tis well we accept them as coming from the chastening hand of God to purify our lives and bring us nearer to Himself. Our night of crucifixion will pass, and then will dawn the glorious morning of our resurrection in God.

O Mary, who stood beneath the Cross of thy Son and sorrowed in union with Him, teach us to love the Cross!

The Five Glorious Mysteries

(For Wednesdays and Saturdays throughout the year, and the Sundays from Easter till Advent.)

The Sorrows of Christ are over. Step by step we have followed Him, mourning over our sins, and weeping for the agony they have caused Him. We have entered the Garden of Gethsemane, heard His three-times repeated prayer, watched the drops of bloody sweat bedewing the ground on which He lay prostrate. The cruel lashes that fell upon His Sacred Body have in a manner cut our souls with bitter pangs for our wrong-doing. Each thorn that pierced His adorable brow has pierced us too and stirred us to thoughts of penance. Sorrowing we have moved towards Calvary mingling our tears with those of Mary, and repenting of the many times when tempted to sin, we have cried: "Away with Jesus of Nazareth; crucify Him, crucify Him." In agony have we stood beneath the Cross, lifting our tear-stained eyes towards Him and hearing Him murmur: "It is consummated." Yes, the work of Redemption is done. The gloom is lifted, the agony has passed. Our day of resurrection is at hand.

First Glorious Mystery:

"The Resurrection"

"And the angel answering said to the women: Fear not you; for I know that you seek Jesus who was crucified. He is not here, for He is risen, as He said. Come and see the place where the Lord was laid."—(St. Matt., XXVIII, 5, 6.)

Rising from Sin

We have learned by bitter experience the sadness of sin; we have learned how evil and bitter a thing it is to have forsaken the Lord our God.

Now, rising from the tomb, Christ teaches the mercy of God. He spoke kindly to the sinful Samaritan woman, He protected the woman taken in sin, He received from the outcast Magdalen tokens of her veneration; yea, from the Cross He spoke words of hope to the penitent thief, and prayed therefrom for every wandering prodigal: "Father, forgive them."

Let us take courage, cast off the old man and put on the new, so that the grace of God may abound in our souls.

O Mary, teach us gratitude to God who has forgiven us!

Second Glorious Mystery:

"The Ascension"

"And He led them out as far as Bethania; and lifting up His hands, He blessed them. And it came to pass, whilst He blessed them, He departed from them, and was carried up to heaven. And they adoring went back to Jerusalem with great joy."—(St. Luke, XXIV, 50, 51, 52.)

Presence of God

"Therefore, if you be risen with Christ, seek the things that are above; where Christ is sitting at the right hand of God. Mind the things that are above, not the things that are upon the earth." (Col. III, 1-2.)

How vile everything earthly appears when compared with the beauty of God, the beauty that shall be revealed by God to them that love Him.

If like the saints of old we "walk with God," seeing a reflection of His loveliness in every beautiful thing in life, and abide in His holy presence at all times by turning every thought, word and deed towards Him, we are learning each moment the lesson of Christ's Ascension. Though now we see "darkly and as in a mirror," we are moving steadily forward toward the Divine revelation when we shall see Him face to face, and shall know even as we are known.

O Mary, teach us always to realize God's holy presence!

Third Glorious Mystery:

"The Descent of the Holy Ghost"

"And when the days of the Pentecost were accomplished, they were all together in one place. And suddenly there came a sound from heaven, as of a mighty wind, and it filled the whole house where they were sitting; and there appeared to them parted tongues as it were of fire, and it sat upon every one of them. And they were all filled with the Holy Ghost."—(Acts, 11, 1-4.)

Hearing God's Voice

To know, to love, to serve God—there is our life's work: to know Him through the works of His hands; to love Him for His tender mercies towards us; to serve Him by obedience to His holy law. In fulfilling the duties of our station in life we are called upon to make sacrifices. Under the guidance of God's spirit let us sacrifice with a good heart, mindful that God loveth a cheerful giver. It may be that God shall say: "Friend, go up higher." "Go sell all that thou hast and give to the poor and come and follow me." Should God summon us to heroic work for His sake, let us obey.

O Mary, spouse of the Holy Spirit, teach us to obey heavenly inspirations!

Fourth Glorious Mystery:

"The Assumption"

"Behold my beloved speaketh to me: Arise, make haste my love, my beautiful one, and come. For winter is now past, the rain is over and gone. The flowers have appeared in our land . . . Arise my love, my beautiful one, and come."—(Canticle of Canticles, II, 10-13.)

Union with God

We have admired Mary's intimate union with her Divine Son, her tender watchfulness, her sweet motherly sympathy, her glorious co-operation in the sacred work of the Redemption. Now that He has ascended into heaven, she cannot endure separation. Her ardent love seeks union with the dear object of her love. By God's will is she borne body and soul to Heaven.

While we are on earth let us strive to be united with God by a bond of charity, which shall increase as the years go on, and find its consummation in the heavenly presence.

O Mary, intense lover of God, teach us to love but God alone!

Fifth Glorious Mystery:

"The Coronation"

"And a great sign appeared in heaven; a woman clothed with the sun, and the moon under her feet, and on her head a crown of twelve stars."—(Apocalypse, XII, 1.)

Perseverance

"He that shall persevere unto the end, he shall be saved" (St. Matt. X., 22). Mary has entered into her reward, and is crowned with glory. We still are in the vale of sorrows, still tempted unto sin. "But God is faithful, who will not suffer you to be tempted above that which you are able: but will make also with temptation issue, that you may be able to bear it." (1 Cor. X., 13.) This thought should steady us in all our trials.

The world may tempt us with its vanities; the flesh may tempt us with its sensualities; the devil may tempt us with his pride; but neither world nor flesh nor devil will be stronger than God's grace that shall be ours in answer to earnest prayer.

O Mary, crowned with glory in Heaven, pray that we may be worthy to be crowned like thee!

We have woven our spiritual crown of roses at the feet of Mary, Queen, our Mother of Mercy, whom, after Jesus, we hail as our life, sweetness and our hope. Mourning and weeping and wandering in vale of tears, still hopefully have we cried to her, knowing that she, our powerful advocate in Heaven, will hear our heart-rending sighs and turn her eyes in love towards us poor banished children of Eve. And when our exile here below is ended the clement, the loving, the sweet Virgin Mother of Jesus, will show us the "Fruit of her womb."

Queen of the Most Holy Rosary, Help of Christians, Refuge of sinners, pray for us, sinners, now and at the hour of our death. Amen.

The Confraternity of the Most Holy Rosary

In the same manner as we believe that the summit of Christian perfection is reached through union with Christ, the fountain of all perfections, and also through the union of Christians among themselves; so in order to attain this perfection we are piously taught that the best means is prayer, and a union and co-operation with our brethren and neighbors in piety and good works. It is for this reason that the Church encourages confraternities, and especially the Rosary Confraternity—the most ancient and universal in the Catholic Church.

Confraternities of the Rosary, established in Dominican Churches, not only enjoy the privileges and indulgences which are common to Confraternities of this character, but also all the privileges, indulgences, favors and concessions granted to any other Confraternity of whatever kind or title. (Benedict XIII, May 26, 1727.) Moreover, the members of the Rosary Confraternity participate, during life and after death, in all the good works, merits and suffrages of the three Orders of St. Dominic.

How to be Admitted into the Confraternity
1. It is necessary to give one's name to a Dominican Priest (or to a Priest who has Dominican faculties).

2. To have one's name entered in the register.
3. To have beads blessed by a Dominican Father (or by a Priest who has Dominican faculties).

All Catholics who have the use of reason can be admitted into the Confraternity. Those absent, the deaf and dumb and the dying can be admitted, provided that they have expressed their desire.

Duties.—The whole fifteen mysteries are to be said by each associate every week; these mysteries may be said separately. Meditation (at the least calling the mystery to mind), is necessary to gain the Indulgences.

The associates do not bind themselves to these duties under any pain of sin; but if the entire Rosary is not said during the week, the member will forfeit many of the Indulgences.

Religious and others who by Rule or pious custom say the Rosary every day, satisfy the obligations of the Confraternity by this recital, and need not say an additional Rosary.

Indulgences of the Rosary Confraternity

The Indulgences of the Rosary, being very many and very great, naturally constitute one of the advantages of membership of the Confraternity. For although some of them may be gained by non-members, only those who have been enrolled in the Confraternity can gain all. Before giving the list of some of these spiritual graces granted by the Church, it is well to bear in mind that the devotion and the Confraternity have existed for nearly seven centuries, and that many Pontiffs have added to the number. It is on record that Pius IX., one day speaking of the innumerable treasures in the palace of the Popes, took his Rosary in his hand and said: "Behold the greatest treasure of the Vatican!"

The Rosary is the greatest treasure of the Vatican because the Vatican has made it so, as the following authentic *List of Indulgences* with their conditions will show:

Part I.
Indulgence Granted to Members Only

I.
ON THE DAY OF ADMISSION.

1. *Plenary.*—On condition of Confession, Communion, reception into Confraternity. (Gregory XIII.)

2. After being received, Confession, Communion in the Church or Chapel of the Confraternity, recitation of Five Mysteries, prayers for the Pope's intentions.

Note.—These Indulgences can be gained either on the day of admission or on the Sunday or Feast day following.

II.
THOSE WHO RECITE THE ROSARY.
(a) During the year.

Plenary.—Once during life, for the weekly recitation of the entire Rosary.

For saying the whole Rosary of Fifteen Mysteries, members gain all the Indulgences granted in Spain to the "Crown of the Blessed Virgin."

50 *years*, once a day, for those reciting Five Mysteries or a third part of the Rosary in the Chapel of the Rosary, or in any part of the Church where the Rosary Altar can be seen. Members who do not live in a place where the Confraternity is erected can gain this Indulgence in any Church or public Oratory. (Adrian VI.)

10 *years* and 10 *forty days* for each recital of the Rosary when said three times in the week. (Leo X.)

7 *years* and 7 *forty days*, once a week, for saying the whole Rosary. It is not necessary to say the whole Rosary at one time. (Pius V.)

5 *years* and 5 *forty days* (i. e. 2025 days) for devoutly pronouncing the Holy Name of Jesus during the recitation of each Hail Mary. (Pius IX. and Leo XIII.)

2 *years* on each of the three times when the whole Rosary is recited during the week.

300 *days* for saying a third part of the Rosary.

100 *days* for inducing others to say a third part of the Rosary.

300 *days*, once a day, for assisting on Sundays or festivals in a Dominican Church, when the Rosary is said or sung processionally before carved or painted representations of each Mystery.

(b) On Certain Days and Feasts.

Plenary.—Feast of the Annunciation; on condition of Confession, Communion and recital of the Rosary. (St. Pius V.)

10 *years* and 10 *forty days* on the Purification, Assumption, Nativity of the Blessed Virgin, for reciting the Rosary.

10 *years* and 10 *forty days* on Easter, Annunciation, Assumption of the Blessed Virgin, for reciting a third part of the Rosary. (St. Pius V.)

7 *years* and 7 *forty days* on the other feasts of our Lord and of the Blessed Virgin on which Mysteries of the Rosary are celebrated, viz.: Visitation of the Blessed Virgin, Christmas Day, Purification, Compassion of the Blessed Virgin (Friday after Passion Sunday), Ascension, Pentecost, and All Saints, for saying at least Five Mysteries. (St. Pius V.)

7 *years* and 7 *forty days* on Christmas Day, the Annunciation, Assumption of the Blessed Virgin, for the usual weekly recitation of the whole Rosary.

100 *days* on the Purification, Annunciation, Visitation, Assumption, Nativity of the Blessed Virgin.

III.
FOR ASSISTING AT THE PROCESSION OF THE ROSARY.

Plenary.—Confession, Communion, assisting at the Procession on the first Sunday of the month, prayers for the Pope's intentions, and visiting the Chapel of the Rosary.

Note.—This Indulgence may be gained by members traveling by sea or land, or who are in service (including soldiers on duty), if they say the entire Rosary; and by those who are sick or legitimately hindered if they recite a third part of the Rosary.

Plenary.—For assisting at the Procession on these feasts of the Blessed Virgin: Purification, Annunciation, Visitation, Assumption, Nativity, Presentation, Immaculate Conception; or on any day within their Octaves.

100 *days* for assisting at the Procession.

60 *days* for assisting at the usual Rosary Procession, or at any other carried out with permission of the Ordinary, or when they accompany the *Viaticum* when it is carried in procession to the sick.

IV.
FOR VISITING THE CHAPEL OR CHURCH OF THE CONFRATERNITY.

Plenary.—First Sunday of the month: On condition of Confession, Communion, visit, with prayers for the Pope's intentions.

Sick members may gain this, after Confession and Communion, by reciting Five Mysteries before a pious image, or by saying the seven penitential psalms.

Plenary.—First Sunday of the month, having received the Sacraments of Penance and Holy Eucharist; prayers before the Blessed Sacrament exposed in the Church of the Confraternity, and prayers for the Pope's intentions.

Plenary.—Visit to the Chapel or Church of the Confraternity; Confession, Communion, prayers for the Pope's intentions between first Vespers and sunset of the following feasts (i e., from about 1 o'clock P. M. of the vigils of these feasts until sunset of the feasts themselves), Christmas, Epiphany, Easter, Ascension, Whitsunday, or any two Fridays in Lent, All Saints, and any day within eight days after All Souls, on Sunday within Octave of Nativity of the Blessed Virgin, on the third Sunday of April.

Plenary.—On same conditions, from first Vespers to sunset of these feasts of the Blessed Virgin, Immaculate Conception, Nativity, Presentation, Annunciation, Visitation, Purification, Assumption; and on one day within the Octave of these feasts; on the Seven Dolorus (Friday after Passion Sunday).

On Easter, Ascension, Whitsunday, on the above feasts of the Blessed Virgin, and on two Fridays in Lent, the Indulgence can be gained by visiting *any* Church or public Chapel.

Travelers by land or sea and those in service can gain the Indulgence for visiting the Church or Chapel of the Rosary on all days on which Mysteries of the Rosary are celebrated, if they recite the entire Rosary (i. e., the Fifteen Mysteries); the sick or legitimately hindered if they say Five Mysteries.

7 *years* and 7 *forty days*, Confession, Communion, visit to Chapel or Altar of the Rosary, with prayers for the Pope's intentions, on Christmas, Easter, Whitsunday, Immaculate Conception, Nativity of the Blessed Virgin, Annunciation, Visitation, Assumption, All Saints.

100 *days, once a day*, for a visit to Chapel or Altar of the Rosary, with prayers for the Pope's intentions.

Note.—Religious women, the inmates of colleges, seminaries, schools and Catholic institutions who are members, can gain all the Indulgences which require a visit to the Chapel or Church of the Confraternity, if they visit their own Church or Chapel.

Sick members and others unable to fulfill the conditions of Communion or visit, can gain the Indulgences if, after Confession and other conditions, they perform some pious work prescribed by their confessor.

For gaining partial Indulgence by the visits, a separate visit is necessary.

V.
FOR VISITING FIVE ALTARS.

For visiting five Altars in any Church or public Oratory (or who five times visit one or two Altars where there are not five), on the appointed days, the same Indulgence as for visiting the Station-Churches in Rome. (Leo X.)

VI.
FOR SAYING OR HEARING THE VOTIVE MASS OF THE ROSARY.

For hearing this Mass and offering some pious prayers, members can gain all the Indulgences granted to the recital of the entire Rosary. Priests who are members gain the same when they say the Mass as prescribed in Churches where the Confraternity is established. Dominican Fathers can say this Mass on all Wednesdays and Saturdays, except on feasts of first and second class, and a few other special days.

Those who are in the habit of celebrating or hearing this Mass gain, once a month, all Indulgences granted for the usual Procession on the first Sunday of the month. Confession and Communion.

1 *year* on Saturdays in Lent for assisting at this Mass and at a Sermon on the Blessed Virgin, and saying the "Hail, Holy Queen."

VII.
FOR THE DEVOTION OF THE FIFTEEN SATURDAYS.
Plenary.—On any three of fifteen consecutive Sundays: Confession, Communion, visit to Church of Confraternity, with prayers for Pope's intentions.
7 *years* and 7 *forty days* on the other twelve Saturdays.

VIII.
FOR DEVOTIONS DURING OCTOBER.
Plenary.—For assisting 10 times at these Devotions in a Dominican Church: Confession, Communion, prayers for Our Holy Father's intentions.
7 *years* and 7 *forty days* each time assisting at the above.

IX.
FOR ASSISTING AT THE SINGING OF THE SALVE REGINA.
3 *years* and 3 *forty days* for assisting at the singing of the "Salve," on certain festivals, in a Church in which the Confraternity exists.
100 *days* for the same every day in the year.
Members who can not assist can gain the Indulgences by kneeling before an Altar or picture of the Blessed Virgin, saying the "Hail, Holy Queen."
40 *days* on all Saturdays and Feasts.

X.
FOR MENTAL PRAYER OR OTHER SPIRITUAL EXERCISES.
Plenary.—Once a month, for at least a quarter of an hour's mental prayer every day for a month: Confession and Communion.
Plenary.—Any one day in the year, for prayer, mortification, and other good works for 40 days, in memory of our Lord's 40 days in the desert.
7 *years* and 7 *forty days* for every half hour of mental prayer.

100 *days* for every quarter of an hour.

XI.
FOR VISITING SICK MEMBERS.
3 *years* and 3 *forty days* for each visit.
100 *days* for inducing them to receive the Sacraments.

XII.
FOR PRAYING FOR DECEASED MEMBERS.
Plenary.—For assisting at the Office of the Dead, which is said in Dominican Churches on the four Anniversaries of the Dead (February 4th., July 12th., September 5th., November 10th.): Confession. Communion, prayers for the Pope's intentions.
8 *years* for assisting at the funeral service and procession on Saturdays, or once a month, in a Church of the Confraternity.
3 *years* and 3 *forty days* following the body of a deceased member to the Church of the Confraternity.
100 *days* for assisting at funerals with the Confraternity Cross, and at anniversaries of deceased members, with prayers for the Pope's intentions.

XIII.
FOR ANY PIOUS WORK.
60 *days* for any work of charity or piety.

XIV.
FOR THE DYING.
Plenary.—Can be applied by any Priest in the usual way, even apart from confession, to all who have been accustomed to say the Rosary every week. (Innocent VIII.)
Plenary.—If having said the entire Rosary at least once, they die holding the blessed candle of the Rosary. (Adrian VI.)
Plenary.—For Confession and Communion.
Plenary.—For invoking the name of JESUS with a contrite heart, if they can not do so with their lips. (Leo XIII.)
Plenary.—After receiving the Sacraments, making an act of faith in the Holy Church, saying the "Hail, Holy Queen," and commending themselves to the Blessed Virgin.
Note.—Any ONE of these Indulgences may be gained, if the

conditions are fulfilled, but not all at the same time.

XV.
FOR THE DEAD.

In all Dominican Churches, the Rosary Altar is privileged for all Fathers of the Order, on behalf of deceased members.

Moreover, the Rosary Altar is always privileged for any Priest, even if not a member, and on behalf of any soul.

Part II.
Indulgences shared in by all the faithful, whether Members of the Confraternity or not.

7 years and 7 *forty days.*—For assisting at the Procession on the first Sunday of the month.

Plenary.—TOTIES QUOTIES. ROSARY SUNDAY. Confession, Communion, visit to the Chapel of the Rosary, or to the Statue of Our Lady, if exposed to veneration in another part of the Church, in honor of the victory of Lepanto gained by the prayers of the Rosary. This Plenary Indulgence may be gained EACH TIME the visit is repeated, from the first Vespers of the feast (that is, from about 1 o'clock on Saturday afternoon) until midnight of Rosary Sunday. During the visits prayers must be said for the Holy Father's intentions. The confession may be made on the Friday or Saturday before Rosary Sunday. (St. Pius V.)

Plenary.—On Corpus Christi, on the feast of the Patron Saint of the Church, and on any day within the Octave of Rosary Sunday: Confession, Communion, visit to the Chapel or Image (as above), with prayers for the Holy Father's intentions.

Note.—All the above Indulgences, except that for the hour of death, can be applied to the Holy Souls.

ADDITIONAL INDULGENCES TO ALL THE FAITHFUL.

Plenary.—Once a year, for Five Mysteries every day, using a Rosary blessed by a Dominican, or by a Priest who has the faculty: Confession and Communion.

100 *days* for each "Our Father" and each "Hail Mary," when saying the entire Rosary, or Five Mysteries on a Rosary blessed as above. (Raccolta, 194.)

5 years and 5 *forty days* for every Five Mysteries or a third part of the Rosary. (Raccolta.)

10 years and 10 *forty days,* once a day, for saying Five Mysteries with others, either at home or in Church, or in a public or private Chapel. (Raccolta.)

Plenary.—Last Sunday of each month, for Five Mysteries three times a week as in the preceding: Confession, Communion, visit any Church or public Chapel, with prayers for the Pope's intentions.

Plenary.—On any one of fifteen consecutive Saturdays, for Five Mysteries or other devotions to the Mysteries of the Rosary: Confession, Communion each Saturday, or on Sundays, if prevented on Saturdays.

7 *years* and 7 *forty days* for the same on the other Saturdays.

Plenary.—For any devout Novena of approved prayers in honor of Our Lady of the Rosary: Contrition, Confession, Communion, prayers for the Pope's intentions on any day within the Novena or within eight days after.

300 *days* on all other days of the above Novena.

FOR OCTOBER DEVOTIONS.

Plenary.—On Rosary Sunday, or any day within the Octave: Confession, Communion, visit to a Church, with prayers for the Pope's intentions; and provided Five Mysteries are said on the feast and on every day during the Octave, either publicly in a Church or in private.

Plenary.—For Five Mysteries, either publicly or in private, on any ten days of October (after the Octave of the Rosary): Confession, Communion, visit to a Church, and there pray for the Pope's intentions, on any day at choice.

7 *years* and 7 *forty days* every day in October for Five Mysteries either in Church or in private.

Note.—All these additional Indulgences are applicable to the Holy Souls.

The above is an exact Summary of Rosary Indulgences as given in the Index of Indulgences, approved by Pope Leo XIII, at an audience granted August 29, 1899.

Since the list just given was approved by Pope Leo XIII, his successor Pope Pius X, added, or rather renewed, an Indulgence formerly granted by Pope Innocent VIII., viz., that of 100 *years and as many forty days* daily to members of the Rosary Confraternity who carry their Rosary beads about with them (July 31, 1906).

A further concession was made by Pope Pius X. (October 13, 1906). To gain the Indulgences attached to the Rosary it is no longer necessary to say the Five Mysteries at one time. They may be separated, and a single Mystery may be said at a time.

CONDITIONS FOR GAINING THE INDULGENCES.

1. The contrition mentioned as required for the gaining of an Indulgence is not an actual condition, but only a necessary disposition, and indicated merely that the recipient must be in the state of grace.

2. Weekly Confession, when habitual, suffices for gaining all the Indulgences, Plenary and Partial, obtainable within the week.

3. One Communion suffices to gain many plenary Indulgences.

4. Communion on Saturday, or on the Vigil of a feast, suffices, provided the other conditions prescribed be performed on the Sunday or feast following.

5. Those unable to receive Holy Communion at the hour of death can gain the Plenary Indulgence in which the condition of Communion is required, by invoking the sacred name of JESUS, at least in heart when they can not do so by word.

6. The visit to the Church, etc., can be made either before or after Communion.

7. The prayers offered in the Indulgenced Church at the time of Mass or Communion suffice for the visit.

8. The Chapels of Convents, Workhouses, Seminaries, etc., may be looked on as public Oratories in favor of those living in them.

9. The Rosary or other prayers prescribed for gaining the above Indulgences need not be said kneeling.

10. The Indulgences granted to members of the Rosary Confraternity are not suspended during the solemn year of the Jubilee, unless special mention of this fact be made in the Papal Bull proclaiming the Jubilee Indulgence.

11. Religious and others who live in colleges, seminaries and schools, and all who live in institutions where they are not free to go out, provided they are members of the Confraternity, may gain the Indulgences for which a visit to the Rosary Chapel or Altar is prescribed, by visiting their own Church or Chapel if they fulfill the others conditions as well.

12. Sick members who can not receive Holy Communion can have that obligation, where prescribed, commuted into some other good work by their confessor, if they go to confession and fulfill the other conditions.

SUMMARY OF INDULGENCES OF DOMINICAN BEADS.

For saying the beads	5,500
For pronouncing devoutly the Holy Name of Jesus	101,250
For saying a third part of the Rosary, each time	2,025
Again for a third part of the Rosary	300
For carrying the beads	40,500
	————
Total (409 *years* and 290 *days* of Indulgences)	149,575
Plus Crozier Indulgence	27,500
	————
	177,075

(485 *years* and 50 *days* of Indulgences.)

CONCLUSION.

We will end with the words of Pope Leo XIII, the venerable and zealous Apostle of the Rosary in the nineteenth century. Speaking to the rulers of the Church, the Pope says: "For these reasons the Roman Pontiffs have ever given the highest praise to this Sodality of our Lady. Innocent VII called it 'a most devout Confraternity.' Pius V declared that by its virtue 'Christians began suddenly to be transformed into other men, the darkness of heresy to be dispelled, and the light of Catholic faith to shine forth.' We also, Venerable Brethren, moved by the example of our predecessors, earnestly exhort and conjure you, as we have often done, to devote special care to this sacred warfare, so that by your efforts fresh forces may be daily enrolled on every side. Through you and those of your clergy who have the care of souls, let the people know and duly appreciate the efficacy of this Sodality and its usefulness for man's salvation." To the faithful laity the Pontiff's fatherly words are no less strong: "For this reason do we exhort all Christians to give themselves to the daily recital of this pious devotion either in public or privately in the home or family of each. We believe it to be in the designs of Providence that, in these times of trials for the Church, the ancient devotion to the august Virgin should live and flourish.

"May the Christian people, excited by our exhortations and inflamed by your appeals, now seek the protection of Mary with an ardor growing greater day by day. Let them betake themselves more and more to the protection of Mary, and trust in Her. Let them cling more and more to the practice of the Rosary, to which our ancestors had recourse as an ever-ready refuge in misfortune, and as a glorious pledge and proof of Christian faith and devotion.

"The heavenly Patroness of the human race will receive with joy these prayers and supplications, and will easily obtain that the good grow in goodness, and that the erring repent and be brought back to salvation; that God, who is the avenger of crime, moved to compassion and mercy, shall deliver Christendom and civil society from their present dangers, and restore to them that peace which is so much desired.

"Encouraged by this hope, we beseech God Himself, with the earnest desire of our heart, to grant you, Venerable Brethren, every gift of heavenly blessing, through Her in whom He has placed the fullness of all grace."

Feast of the Most Holy Name of Mary, September, 1915.

www.ingramcontent.com/pod-product-compliance
Lightning Source LLC
Chambersburg PA
CBHW031249130726
47988CB00008B/3309

* 9 7 9 8 8 6 9 3 1 2 0 3 7 *